ANGEL COMMUNICATION

See, Hear and Feel the Angels

Emeka Ejinkonye, PhD

DEDICATION

To my wife Elizabeth for her understanding

and my children Joshua, Elizabeth (junior),

Sharon and David

.

LEGAL NOTICE
The Publisher has strived to be as accurate and complete as possible in the creation of this report, notwithstanding the fact that he does not warrant or represent at any time that the contents within are accurate due to the rapidly changing nature of theological and philosophical discoveries around the world.

While all attempts have been made to verify information provided in this publication, the Publisher assumes no responsibility for errors, omissions, or contrary interpretation of the subject Matter herein. Any perceived slights of specific persons, peoples, or organizations are unintentional.

In practical advice books, like anything else in life, there are no guarantees of income made. Readers are cautioned to reply on their own judgment about their individual circumstances to act accordingly.

This book is not intended for use as a source of legal, business, accounting or financial advice. All readers are advised to seek services of competent professionals in legal, business, accounting and finance fields.

May God bless you, grant you the fortitude and resilience to know that the best is yet to come.

CONTENTS

Introduction

We hear stories of Angels in many religions of the world. Throughout the ages, people of different clans, tribe, cultures **and civilisations** are intrigued about these extra-terrestrial beings. Angel stories are always fascinating and there are good Angels, the bad Angels, and the ugly Angels.

The good angels are the holy ones, the bad angels are the evil ones, which the Scriptures address as demons, and the ugly angels are demons of deception, disguising themselves as good Angels. These ugly Angels have deceived many people in a culture that has embraced "Angel mania."

Many people **often** assume when it comes to the angelic realm. They chaotically base their beliefs on what they've always heard or what sounds good. The truth about angels has been twisted and distorted into a confusing assortment of fables and myths.

People have wanted their senses titillated, and they like to hear smooth things that lack true spiritual substance. So often there is a constant barrage of falsehood, against which even true believers must guard their thoughts, actions and beliefs.

Do Angels exist? What are Angels? Do Angels help people? Are Angels visible? Will people become Angels in heaven? Do Angels fly? Do Angels have wings? Are all Angels good? What is the job of an Angel? Are there Guardian Angels? Can we worship Angels? What will Angels do at judgment? Are Angels immortal? Where do Angels come from?

These are just some of the questions that people have about Angels which I intend to address in this book. People are always talking about angels; about having guardian angels.

Many movies have been made about angels and how angels get their wings. The one thing that we can learn about angels from man is that he doesn't really know what he is talking about.

Man has a thought process that leaves out the Scriptures and the things that God has told us. So, if we want to find out about angels we must go to God's word.

There are some right ideas among the various portrayals and descriptions but also many misconceptions which I aspire to put right by the angelic guidance.

An Angel of the Lord telling Mary about the envisaged birth of our Lord and Saviour Jesus Christ.

For the truth about angels we must turn to the God who made them and made everything else as well. And what He says is found in His Word - the Holy Scriptures. What then, does the Scripture actually say about Angels?

ACKNOWLEDGMENTS

First I want to give thanks to God for protection
and the ability to do this work

I want to say thanks to all who contributed in one way
or another to completion of this book.

Special thanks to my young theologian Sharon for proof reading,

and to David for his technical and graphic design contributions.

1 EXISTENCE AND APPEARANCE OF ANGELS

Where do angels come from?

Angels are beings who have greater power and ability than humans. (2 Peter 2:11) They exist in heaven, or the spirit realm, which is a level of existence higher than the physical universe. (1 Kings 8:27; John 6:38) Thus, they are also referred to as spirits.- *1 Kings 22:21; Psalm 18:10*.

Angels are certainly real; the Bible repeatedly tells us about them, and the work God has given them to do. They are spiritual beings, the Bible says, who were created by God to do His will. The Bible says, "Are not all angels ministering spirits sent to serve those who will inherit salvation?" (*Hebrews 1:14*).

Angels were created in the distant past, before the earth existed. When God created the earth, the angels "began shouting in applause." - *Job 38:4-7*.

God created the angels through Jesus, whom the Bible calls "the firstborn of all creation." Describing how God used Jesus in creation, the Bible says: "By means of [Jesus] all other things were created in the heavens and on the earth, the things visible and the things invisible," including the angels. (Colossians 1:13-17)

Angels do not marry and reproduce. (Mark 12:25) Instead, each of these "sons of the true God" was individually created.(Job 1:6)

Angels are invisible
Because they are spiritual and not physical beings, the angels usually are invisible and unseen by us. In fact, one of heaven's joys, I believe, will be the joy of looking back over our lives and discovering just how often the angels intervened to save us or bless us -although we weren't even aware of it at the time. The Psalmist said that God "will command his angels concerning you to guard you in all your ways" *(Psalm 91:11)*.

Nevertheless, the Bible also tells us that at times the angels have become visible. When God announced to the Virgin Mary that she would bear His Son, He used the angel Gabriel to convey the news to her (see Luke 1:26-38).

When Jesus' birth was announced to the shepherds outside Bethlehem, "a great company of the heavenly host appeared … praising God" (Luke 2:13). Many other examples from the Bible could be cited.

Do angels still appear?
I'm convinced they do on occasion — although sometimes we may not even be aware of them, because they have chosen to appear as ordinary human beings.

We should thank God for His Angels, but at the same time, we shouldn't become overly preoccupied with them; Nor should we worship them, for only God - Father, Son and Holy Spirit - is worthy of our worship.

How do Angels look like?

The Bible doesn't tell us exactly what angels look like; in fact, they often are invisible to us, because they are spiritual beings who seldom take on any physical appearance.

At times, however, they do become visible. When the prophet Isaiah was given a vision of God's majesty and glory, His throne was surrounded by angels. They were similar in appearance to humans, with faces and feet, but they also had wings and could fly (see Isaiah 6:1-3).

When the angel announced Jesus' birth to the shepherds outside Bethlehem, the Bible says that "the glory of the Lord shone around them" (Luke 2:9). On the other hand, angels sometimes took the appearance of ordinary men, and were only recognized as Angels later (see, for example, Genesis 19).

God created the angels before the beginning of time, and they had one purpose: to be God's servants. Today, angels continually watch over God's people, to deliver them from evil and safeguard their entrance into heaven.

We may not even think about them very much or realise their importance, but they still watch over us — and we should thank God for them. The Bible says, "Are not all angels ministering spirits sent to serve those who will inherit salvation?" *(Hebrews 1:14)*.

The angels' work on our behalf should remind us of God's love for us. At the same time, we are not to worship the angels or give undue attention to them. Christ alone is our Saviour, and He alone is the One to whom we should look for our salvation. Have you put your faith and trust in Him?

Angels appeared as human
Let mutual loves continue. Do not neglect to show hospitality to strangers, for by doing that some have entertained angels without knowing it. *Hebrews 13:1-2.*

And he lifts up his eyes and looked, and, lo, three men stood by him: and when he saw them, he ran to meet them from the tent door, and bowed himself toward the ground. *Genesis 18:2*

 And there came two angels to Sodom at even; and Lot sat in the gate of Sodom: and Lot seeing them rose up to meet them; and he bowed himself with his face toward the ground. *Genesis 19:1*

Can people see Angels?
Then Elisha prayed: "O LORD, please open his eyes that he may see." So the LORD opened the eyes of the servant, and he saw; the mountain was full of horses and chariots of fire all around Elisha. *2 Kings 6:17.*

The donkey saw the angel of the LORD standing in the road, with a drawn sword in his hand. Thus the donkey turned off the road, and went into the field and Balaam struck the donkey, to turn it back onto the road. *Numbers 22:23.*

The Angel appeared like lightening with cloths as white as snow
Muslims believe that God created angels from light.
The **Hadith,** a traditional collection of information about **the prophet Muhammad,** declares: "The angels were created from light …".

Christians and **Jewish people** often describe angels as glowing with light from within as a physical manifestation of **the passion for God that is burning within angels**.

In **Buddhism** and **Hinduism**, angels are described as having the essence of light, even though they're often depicted in art as having human or even animal bodies. The angelic beings of Hinduism are considered to be minor gods called "**devas**," which means "shining ones."

During near-death experiences (NDEs), people often report meeting angels who appear to them in the form of light and lead them through tunnels toward **a greater light that some believe may be God**.

Auras and Halos

Some people think that the **halos that Angels wear** in traditional artistic depictions of them are actually parts of **their light-filled auras** (the energy fields that surround them).

William Booth, the founder of the <u>Salvation Army</u>, reported seeing a group of angels surrounded by an aura of extremely bright light in all **colours** of the rainbow.

UFOs

The mysterious lights reported as **unidentified flying objects** (UFOs) throughout the world at various times may be Angels, say some people.

Those who believe that UFOs could be Angels say their beliefs are consistent with some accounts of Angels in religious scriptures.

For example, Genesis 28:12 of both the Torah and the Bible describes Angels using a celestial staircase to ascend and descend from the sky.

Angel speaking to Mary at the tomb was consistent in the four Gospel accounts

1. (Matthew 28:6-7) - "He is not here, for He has risen, just as He said. Come, see the place where He was lying. And go quickly and tell His disciples that He has risen from the dead; and behold, He is going before you into Galilee, there you will see Him; behold, I have told you."

2. (Mark 16:6-7) - "And he *said to them, "Do not be amazed; you are looking for Jesus the Nazarene, who has been crucified. He has risen; He is not here; behold, here is the place where they laid Him. "But go, tell His disciples and Peter, 'He is going before you into Galilee; there you will see Him, just as He said to you.'"

3. (Luke 24:5-7) - "and as the women were terrified and bowed their faces to the ground, the men said to them, "Why do you seek the living One among the dead? "He is not here, but He has risen. Remember how He spoke to you while He was still in Galilee, saying that the Son of Man must be delivered into the hands of sinful men, and be crucified, and the third day rise again."

4. (John 20:13) - "And they *said to her, "Woman, why are you weeping?" She *said to them, "Because they have taken away my Lord, and I do not know where they have laid Him."

Angels spoke to the people at Jesus' ascension
After he said this, he was taken up before their very eyes, and a cloud hid him from their sight. They were looking intently up into the sky as he was going, when suddenly two men dressed in white stood beside them.

"Men of Galilee," they said, "why do you stand here looking into the sky? This same Jesus, who has been taken from you into heaven, will come back in the same way you have seen him go into heaven." *Acts 1: 9 - 11*

Angels appeared like flying entity

Above him were seraphs, each with six wings: With two wings they covered their faces, with two they covered their feet, and with two they were flying. *Isaiah 6:2*

Do Angels have wings?

The most common picture of an angel is essentially a human being with wings. This is not scriptural. The Bible frequently presents angels as appearing as humans.

Nevertheless, this does not show that angels in their essence resemble human beings. Further, the Bible very seldom explains angels as having wings. Nevertheless, there are two kinds of angels discussed in the Bible that have wings:

Above him were seraphs, each with six wings: With two wings they covered their faces, with two they covered their feet, and with two they were flying. And they were calling to one another: "Holy, Holy, Holy is the Lord Almighty; the whole earth is full of His glory." *Isaiah 6:2-3*

Cherubim and seraphim are 2 kinds of angels, potentially the 2 greatest orders of angels with wings. Exodus 25:19 - 20 recorded "Make one cherub on the one end, and one cherub on the other end. Of one piece with the mercy seat shall you make the cherubim on its two ends.

The cherubim shall spread out their wings above, overshadowing the mercy seat with their wings, their faces one to another; toward the mercy seat shall the faces of the cherubim be." From the above, it may be safe to say that some angels do have wings.

Angels are innumerable
The Bible does not give an exact figure, but it does show that their number is vast. For example, a vision given to the apostle John included a glimpse of hundreds of millions of angels.—Revelation 5:11

An Angel of the Lord telling the High Priest Zechariah about the envisaged birth of John the Baptist

Angels seem to have names

Yes. The Bible gives the names of two angels: Michael and Gabriel. (Daniel 12:1; Luke 1:26) * Other angels acknowledged that they had names, but they did not reveal them. Jacob's encounter with the Angel of God was recorded as follows "

'Your name will no longer be Jacob," the man told him. "From now on you will be called Israel, because you have fought with God and with men and have won." "Please tell me your name," Jacob said. "Why do you want to know my name?" the man replied. Then he blessed Jacob there.' *Genesis 32:29;*

Another interesting story about Angels withholding their names was recorded in the thirteen chapter of the book of Judges.

A certain man of Zorah, named Manoah, from the clan of the Danites, had a wife who was childless, unable to give birth. The angel of the LORD appeared to her and said, "You are barren and childless, but you are going to become pregnant and give birth to a son.

Now see to it that you drink no wine or other fermented drink and that you do not eat anything unclean. You will become pregnant and have a son whose head is never to be touched by a razor because the boy is to be a Nazirite, dedicated to God from the womb.

He will take the lead in delivering Israel from the hands of the Philistines." Then the woman went to her husband and told him, "A man of God came to me. He looked like an angel of God, very awesome.

I didn't ask him where he came from, and he didn't tell me his name. But he said to me, 'You will become pregnant and have a son. Now then, drink no wine or other fermented drink and do not eat anything unclean, because the boy will be a Nazirite of God from the womb until the day of his death.'"

Then Manoah prayed to the LORD: "Pardon your servant, Lord. I beg you to let the man of God you sent to us come again to teach us how to bring up the boy who is to be born."

God heard Manoah's prayer, and the Angel came again to the woman while she was out in the field; but her husband Manoah was not with her. The woman hurried to tell her husband, "He's here! The man who appeared to me the other day!"

Manoah got up and followed his wife. When he came to the man, he said, "Are you the man who talked to my wife?" "I am," he said.

So Manoah asked him, "When your words are fulfilled, what is to be the rule that governs the boy's life and work?"

The Angel of the LORD answered, "Your wife must do all that I have told her. She must not eat anything that comes from the grapevine, nor drink any wine or other fermented drink nor eat anything unclean. She must do everything I have commanded her."

Manoah said to the angel of the LORD, "We would like you to stay until we prepare a young goat for you." The angel of the LORD replied, "Even though you detain me, I will not eat any of your food.

But if you prepare a burnt offering, offer it to the LORD." (Manoah did not realize that it was the Angel of the LORD.)

Then Manoah inquired of the Angel of the LORD, "What is your name, so that we may honor you when your word comes true?" He replied, "Why do you ask my name? It is beyond understanding." Judges 13:17 - 18.

The woman gave birth to a boy and named him Samson. He grew and the LORD blessed him, and the Spirit of the LORD began to stir him.

Angels have distinct personalities. They can communicate with one another. (1 Corinthians 13:1) They have thinking ability and are able to compose expressions of praise to God. (Luke 2:13, 14)

And they have the freedom to choose between right and wrong, as seen when some of them sinned by joining Satan the Devil in his rebellion against God - Matthew 25:41; 2 Peter 2:4.

What is the difference between Guardian Angel and Spirit Guide?
If you have spent some time around the New Age people or in spiritual development circles, you will surely come across terms like *spirit guides* and *guardian angels;* many people use these terms interchangeably.

In reality, they are not the same. A spirit Guide is not an Angel, and there are many levels of angelic beings, as explained in second chapter.

Many people are fascinated with the concept of spirit guides and angels. I would like to explain the difference in the following way.

What is a Spirit Guide?

We all have spirit guides. You have at least one guide who is always present to assist you. A spirit guide is considered a soul that has attained a certain stage in their evolution so that they have sufficient knowledge and awareness to assist another soul in their evolution.

Guides were once incarnated as humans, so they have good understanding of human experience. Spirit guides have consciously and purposely taken on the role of being a guide. They want to assist you; it's their job! They can't intervene in your life unless you ask.

I encourage you to find a way to cultivate a relationship with them or at least to develop a greater awareness of them. You can consider spirit guides as a friend with greater wisdom and unconditional love.

They guide us through different ages and stages of life. Spirit guides usually perform different tasks in our life – acting as personal confidante, helping with healing, emotional issues and spiritually.

Some people work with their spirit guides to help them excel in their career, or to improve in to specific sphere of life.

What is a Guardian Angel?

Different religious bodies or spiritual traditions tend to depict the angelic realms in different ways. There seems to be agreement that there is a hierarchy of angels see chapter two.

Similar to spirit guides, guardian angels are on-hand to guide and protect us from turbulence and complexities of life. Angels are the embodiment of unconditional love, compassion, and wisdom.

Angels are heavenly creatures living in the realms of the spirit, they have never been incarnated, but have the ability to transform into another being in order to accomplish a specific assignment.

One can communicate with angels in many different ways but always remember that they are not to be worshiped.

CHAPTER TWO - ANGELIC HIERACHY

Angels are a class of spiritual beings created by God. Praise the Lord! Praise the Lord from the heavens; Praise Him in the heights! Praise Him, all His angels; Praise Him, all His hosts! Praise Him, sun and moon; Praise Him, all you stars of light! Praise Him, you heavens of heavens. And you waters above the heavens! Let them praise the name of the Lord. For He commanded and they were created - **Psalm 148:1-5 – God created them.**

Throughout time, millions of people have felt the grace, guidance and protection of Angels. Races and cultures around the world have association with these intriguing celestial beings.

Abraham Lincoln often called upon the healing powers and wisdom of the Angels to help guide him and heal in times of personal or national challenges.

George Washington spoke of his Guardian Angel often and credited his success at Valley Forge to "an inspiring visit from a heavenly being."

Angels have an order in their ranks. Below are the three spheres of Angelic core. Every sphere has in it three categories of Angels.

1First Sphere

- 1.1 Seraphim
- 1.2 Cherubim
- 1.3 Thrones

2 Second Sphere

- 2.1 Dominions or Lordships
- 2.2 Virtues or Strongholds
- 2.3 Powers or Authorities

3 Third Sphere

- 3.1 Principalities or Rulers
- 3.2 Archangels
- 3.3 Angels
  - 3.3.1Personal guardian angels

We may be able to speak directly to God through prayer, but according to the Bible, he reaches us through a variety of **angels**, each with distinct duties. There are nine types of angels within three major groups known as choirs. Regardless of where they are on the hierarchy, like us, they are individuals.

Unlike us, because they are able to see far beyond a mortal timeline, they are extremely patient and forgiving. They are aware of our personal life goals and are assigned to assist us, but never interfere with our free will. The first choir, in its celestial form, is represented by wavelengths of light and force fields and frequencies of sound. These entities emanate vibrations, or waves, of devotional love into the universe.

SERAPHIM are the highest order of the Hierarchy of Angels. These angelic beings spend their time worshiping and praising God. The prophet Isaiah vividly describes them in his vision of God: He quotes: In the year that King Uzziah died, I saw the Lord sitting on a throne, high and lifted up, and the train of His robe filled the temple.

Above it stood seraphim; each one had six wings: with two he covered his face, with two he covered his feet, and with two he flew. And one cried to another and said: 'Holy, holy, holy is the Lord of hosts; the whole earth is full of His glory!(Isaiah 6:1-3).

CHERUBIM are the second highest order. The Bible depicts Cherubim as powerful and majestic angelic creatures who surround God's throne (see Ezekiel I :5 – I 4; 28: I 2). They are also depicted on the Ark of the Covenant as its Guardians.

God sent them to guard Eden after the expulsion of Adam and Eve: After He drove the man out, He placed on the east side of the Garden of Eden cherubim and a flaming sword flashing back and forth to guard the way to the tree of life. *(Genesis :24).*

THRONES are the third ranking order of angels. They were also known as Wheels and the Many-eyed Ones. These Angels were often believed to be deployed like charioteers around the Throne of God. They were described in Ezekiel 1:13-19 as having four wings and four faces.

They sparkled like the colour of barnished brass. They had the hands of a man under their wings. Their wings were joined one to the other and they did not turn when they travelled -they all went straight forward. They had four faces. They had the face of a man as well as three other faces on their helmets – that of a lion, an ox, and an eagle.

They moved on wheels in the middle of wheels, blue-green in colour. Above their heads the likeness of the firmament, which was the colour of crystal, and under this were their wings, two on each side of their bodies. The noise of their wings was like the noise of great waters.

DOMINIONS are the fourth ranking order of angels. This Order of Guardian Angels decide the success or failure of nations. Dominations have been described as wearing long albs, or gowns reaching to their feet, hitched with a golden belt and adorned with a green sole. They carry golden staffs in the right hand and the Seal of God in the left. At other times, they are said to hold an orb or a spectre.

VIRTUES are the fifth ranking Order of Angels. They have been called "The Brilliant or Shining Ones. They were called the Angels of miracles, encouragement, and blessings. They were particularly involved with people struggling with their faith.

Virtues have been said to be the chief bestowers of grace and valour. The two Angels at the Ascension of Jesus were traditionally believed to be from the Order of Virtues. Virtues were usually represented in a group.

POWERS are the sixth ranking Order of Angels. Powers have been credited as being the first Order of Angels created by God. They are responsible for maintaining the border between Heaven and Earth.

Acting as a sort of elite guard, they constantly watch for demonic attack. They are the major line of defence and battle during heavenly warfare. It is their duty to protect the world from the infiltration of demons.

They protect our souls from these evil beings and act as ministers of God who avenge evil in the world. It was also believed that at death, the Powers guide our transition to Heaven.

PRINCIPALITIES OR PRINCES are the seventh ranking Order of Angels. The Principalities were considered to be the guardians over the nations and the leaders of the world. It is believed that they are given more freedom to act than the lesser angels below them.

They are responsible for carrying out divine acts concerning their area of jurisdiction. It was from this Order that the Angel who aided David in his task of slaying Goliath was thought to have come. Finally, they are given to the task of managing the duties of the angels. Principalities have been described as being dressed in soldier's uniforms with golden girdles.

ARCHANGELS are eighth ranking order of angels. Archangel Michael is believed to be the highest ranking warring angel in God's heavenly host. He will play a special role in the end time:

For the Lord Himself will come down from heaven, with a loud command, with the voice of the archangel and with the trumpet call of God, and the dead in Christ will rise first.

After that, we who are still alive and are left will be caught up together with them in the clouds to meet the Lord in the air. And so we will be with the Lord forever. (1 Thessalonians 4:16-1 7). As powerful as Michael is, he does keep to his proper domain (Jude 1:6) and does not over-exert his authority over his adversary, Lucifer.

But even the archangel Michael, when he was disputing with the devil about the body of Moses, did not dare to bring a slanderous accusation against him. He said, 'The Lord rebuke you!(Jude I: 9).Ultimately, however, Scripture says that he will prevail over Satan (see Revelation 12: 79).

Archangel Gabriel is a highest-ranking messenger who brought special messages to God's people. In the Scripture we find him bringing messages to: Daniel to reveal the future events to him (Daniel 8:16; 9:21).

He went to Zacharias regarding the birth of John the Baptist, (Luke 1:19) and to Mary to announce the birth of Jesus (Luke I :30).

ANGELS are the last order of angels. They are believed to be ministering angels sent forth to minister for those who will inherit salvation (Hebrews 1:14). Within the orders of angels, only archangels and angels (the lowest categories in the hierarchy) are traditionally said to interact with man and woman in the course of daily life.

In some cases, the angel serves only as a messenger, but in others, the angel lingers in visible form, taking responsibility for the well-being of individuals in trouble, guarding them from harm, offering them sustenance, or leading them out of danger. Nowadays they are still busy ministering to us.

3 NATURE OF ANGELS

Are angels to be worshipped?
Angels are not meant to be worshiped. Whenever Angels are mistaken for God by humans and worshiped in the Bible, they are told not to do this.

And I fell at his feet to worship him. But he said to me, "See that you do not do that! I am your fellow servant, and of your brethren who have the testimony of Jesus. <u>Worship God</u>! For the testimony of Jesus is the spirit of prophecy." (*Revelation 19:10, NKJV*)

Angelic Misconceptions

Misconception: All angels are good.

Fact: The Bible refers to "the wicked spirit forces" and "the angels who sinned." (Ephesians 6:12; 2 Peter 2:4) These wicked angels are **demons**, who joined Satan in rebelling against God. So kindly note that not all angels are good.

Misconception: Angels are immortal.
Fact: Wicked angels, including Satan the Devil, will be destroyed.—Jude 6.

In my opinion, they are. I believe that Jesus addressed this issue in Luke 20:35-36, when he said, "But those who are counted worthy to attain that age, and the resurrection from the dead, neither marry nor are given in marriage; nor can they die anymore, for they are equal to the angels and are sons of God, being sons of the resurrection."

This passage of the scripture tends to suggest that Angels are immortal. But Hebrews 2:14 speaks of God destroying the devil, but my understanding is that the Greek word (Anglicised as "katargese") that is translated as "destroy" in the King James Version rendering of this passage also means "to break the power of", as multiple modern translations express it.

They will be made permanently ineffectual, and no longer able to oppose God, or to deceive or otherwise afflict the redeemed, but they will not be destroyed.) There is some controversy in the translation concerning the mortality of these spiritual beings – the Lucifer and his demons.

Misconception: People become angels when they die.
Fact: Angels are a separate creation of God, not resurrected humans. God created humans differently from Angels. (Colossians 1:16) People who are raised to life in heaven receive the gift of immortal life from God. (1 Corinthians 15:53, 54) They will have a status higher than the angels.— 1 Corinthians 6:3.

Misconception: Angels exist to serve humans.
Fact: Angels obey God's commands, not ours. (Psalm 103:20, 21)

Even Jesus acknowledged that He would call on God for help, not directly on the angels.—Matthew 2_6:53.

Misconception: We can pray to angels for help.

Fact: Prayer to God is part of our worship, which belongs to Jehovah God. (Revelation 19:10) We should **pray only to** God, through Jesus.—John 14:6.

4 FUNCTIONS OF ANGELS

Each of the four living creatures had six wings and was
covered with eyes all around, even under its wings. Day and
night they never stop saying:

"'Holy, holy, holy

is the Lord God Almighty,'

who was, and is, and is to come."

Whenever the living creatures give glory, honour and thanks
to him who sits on the throne and who lives forever and
ever, the twenty-four elders fall down before him who sits on
the throne and worship him who lives forever and ever. They
lay their crowns before the throne and say:

"You are worthy, our Lord and God,
    to receive glory and honour and power,
for you created all things,
    and by your will they were created
    and have their being." *Revelation 4:8– 11*

And again, when God brings his firstborn into the world, He
said,

"Let all God's angels worship him." *Hebrews 1:6*

Do angels help people?

Yes, God uses His faithful Angels to help people today.

- Angels are used by God as He directs His servants in the preaching of the Good News of the <u>Kingdom of God</u> Revelation 14:6, 7. This direction benefits both those preaching and those hearing the good news.—*Acts 8:26, 27.*
- Angels help to keep the Christian congregation free of contamination by wicked people.—*Matthew 13:49.*
- Angels guide and protect those who are faithful to God.—*Psalm 34:7; 91:10, 11; Hebrews 1:7, 14.*
- Soon, the angels will bring relief to mankind by fighting alongside Jesus Christ to eliminate wickedness.—*2 Thessalonians 1:6-8.*

Do we each have a guardian angel?

Although angels look out for the spiritual welfare of God's servants, this does not necessarily mean that God assigns an angel to each Christian as a personal guardian (**Matthew 18:10**).

Angels do not protect God's servants from every trial or temptation. The Bible shows that God will often "make the way out" of a trial by giving a person the wisdom and strength to endure.—*1 Corinthians 10:12, 13; James 1:2-5.*

Other areas of Scriptures highlighting angelic functions include:

Elijah Flees to Horeb

Now Ahab told Jezebel everything Elijah had done and how he had killed all the prophets with the sword. So Jezebel sent a messenger to Elijah to say, "May the gods deal with me, be it ever so severely, if by this time tomorrow I do not make your life like that of one of them." *1 Kings 19:1 – 18*

Sodom and Gomorrah Destroyed

In the Genesis account, God reveals to Abraham that **Sodom and Gomorrah** are to be destroyed for their grave sins (18:20). Abraham pleads for the lives of any righteous people living there, especially the lives of his nephew, Lot, and his family.

The two angels arrived at Sodom in the evening, and Lot was sitting in the gateway of the city. When he saw them, he got up to meet them and bowed down with his face to the ground.

"My lords," he said, "please turn aside to your servant's house. You can wash your feet and spend the night and then go on your way early in the morning."

"No," they answered, "we will spend the night in the square."

But he insisted so strongly that they did go with him and entered his house. He prepared a meal for them, baking bread without yeast, and they ate.

Before they had gone to bed, all the men from every part of the city of Sodom - both young and old -surrounded the house.

They called to Lot, "Where are the men who came to you tonight? Bring them out to us so that we can have sex with them." *Genesis 19: 1 - 5*

Isaac and Rebecca

According to Genesis chapters twenty-four to twenty-seven. Isaac was the son of Abraham and Sarah, promised by God and born to them late in life. When Isaac was of age to be married, Abraham called for his most dependable servant and bestowed upon him a crucial role in this story.

He commanded the servant to search out and find his son a wife from a good family that would join him in devotion to God.

The servant travelled to a town called Nahor and stopped by a well to pray, "Lord, God of my master Abraham, make me successful today and show kindness to my master Abraham. See, I am standing beside this spring and the daughters of the townspeople are coming out to draw water.

May it be that when I say to a young woman, 'please let down your jar that I may have a drink,' and she says, 'Drink, and I'll water your camels too'-let her be the one you have chosen for your servant Isaac. By this, I will know that you have shown kindness to my master."

Angels Prepare the Way

See I am sending an angel ahead of you to guard you along the way and to bring you to the place I have prepared. Pay attention to him and listen to what he says. Do not rebel against him; he will not forgive your rebellion, since my Name is in him.

If you listen carefully to what he says and do all that I say, I will be an enemy to your enemies and will oppose those who oppose you.

My angel will go ahead of you and bring you into the land of the Amorites, Hittites, Perizzites, Canaanites, Hivites and Jebusites, and I will wipe them out. Do not bow down before their gods or worship them or follow their practices.

You must demolish them and break their sacred stones to pieces. Worship the LORD your God and his blessing will be on your food and water. I will take away sickness from among you, and none will miscarry or be barren in your land. I will give you a full life span.

"I will send my terror ahead of you and throw into confusion every nation you encounter. I will make all your enemies turn their backs and run. I will send the hornet ahead of you to drive the Hivites, Canaanites and Hittites out of your way.

But I will not drive them out in a single year, because the land would become desolate and the wild animals too numerous for you. Little by little I will drive them out before you, until you have increased enough to take possession of the land.

"I will establish your borders from the Red Sea to the Mediterranean Sea, and from the desert to the Euphrates River. I will give into your hands the people who live in the land, and you will drive them out before you. Do not make a covenant with them or with their gods. Do not let them live in your land or they will cause you to sin against me, because the worship of their gods will certainly be a snare to you."
Exodus 23: 20 - 32

Destruction of Sodom and Gomorrah

Sodom and Gomorrah were two cities mentioned in the deuterocanonical books, as well as in the Quran and the Hadith.

Torah, recorded that the kingdoms of Sodom and Gomorrah were allied with the cities of Admah, Zeboim, and Bela.

In the book of Genesis, God reveals to Abraham that **Sodom and Gomorrah** are to be **destroyed** for their sexual perversion (18:20). ...

Two angels are sent to Lot in **Sodom** but are met with a wicked mob who demand ed to have homosexual affairs with them but were then struck blind by the angelic guests (19:1–11).

The fall of Jericho
The Wall of **Jericho** was destroyed when the Israelites walked around it for seven days carrying the Ark of the Covenant. On the seventh day, Joshua commanded his people to blow their trumpets made of rams' horns and shout at the walls until they finally fell down
Joshua 5:13-6:27

Jesus Is Tested in the Wilderness
Then Jesus was led by the Spirit into the wilderness to be tempted by the devil. After fasting forty days and forty nights, he was hungry. The tempter came to him and said, "If you are the Son of God, tell these stones to become bread."

Jesus answered, "It is written: 'Man shall not live on bread alone, but on every word that comes from the mouth of God.'"

Then the devil took him to the holy city and had him stand on the highest point of the temple. "If you are the Son of God," he said, "throw yourself down. For it is written:

"'He will command his angels concerning you,
    and they will lift you up in their hands,
    so that you will not strike your foot against a stone.'"
Jesus answered him, "It is also written: 'Do not put the Lord your God to the test.'"

Again, the devil took him to a very high mountain and showed him all the kingdoms of the world and their splendour. "All this I will give you," he said, "if you will bow down and worship me."

Jesus said to him, "Away from me, Satan! For it is written: 'Worship the Lord your God, and serve him only.'"

Then the devil left him, and angels came and attended him. *Matthew 4: 1 - 11*

The Apostles Persecuted

Then the high priest and all his associates, who were members of the party of the Sadducees, were filled with jealousy. They arrested the apostles and put them in the public jail.

But during the night an angel of the Lord opened the doors of the jail and brought them out. "Go, stand in the temple courts," he said, "and tell the people all about this new life."

At daybreak they entered the temple courts, as they had been told, and began to teach the people. When the high priest and his associates arrived, they called together the Sanhedrin—the full assembly of the elders of Israel—and sent to the jail for the apostles.

But on arriving at the jail, the officers did not find them there. So they went back and reported, "We found the jail securely locked, with the guards standing at the doors; but when we opened them, we found no one inside."

On hearing this report, the captain of the temple guard and the chief priests were at a loss, wondering what this might lead to.

Then someone came and said, "Look! The men you put in jail are standing in the temple courts teaching the people." At that, the captain went with his officers and brought the apostles.

They did not use force, because they feared that the people would stone them. The apostles were brought in and made to appear before the Sanhedrin to be questioned by the high priest.

"We gave you strict orders not to teach in this name," he said. "Yet you have filled Jerusalem with your teaching and are determined to make us guilty of this man's blood."

Peter and the other apostles replied: "We must obey God rather than human beings! The God of our ancestors raised Jesus from the dead—whom you killed by hanging him on a cross.

God exalted him to his own right hand as Prince and Saviour that he might bring Israel to repentance and forgive their sins. We are witnesses of these things, and so is the Holy Spirit, whom God has given to those who obey him."

When they heard this, they were furious and wanted to put them to death. But a Pharisee named Gamaliel, a teacher of the law, who was honored by all the people, stood up in the Sanhedrin and ordered that the men be put outside for a little while.

Then he addressed the Sanhedrin: "Men of Israel, consider carefully what you intend to do to these men. Some time ago Theudas appeared, claiming to be somebody, and about four hundred men rallied to him. He was killed, all his followers were dispersed, and it all came to nothing.

After him, Judas the Galilean appeared in the days of the census and led a band of people in revolt. He too was killed, and all his followers were scattered. Therefore, in the present case I advise you: Leave these men alone! Let them go!

For if their purpose or activity is of human origin, it will fail. But if it is from God, you will not be able to stop these men; you will only find yourselves fighting against God."

His speech persuaded them. They called the apostles in and had them flogged. Then they ordered them not to speak in the name of Jesus, and let them go. The apostles left the Sanhedrin, rejoicing because they had been counted worthy of suffering disgrace for the Name.

Day after day, in the temple courts and from house to house, they never stopped teaching and proclaiming the good news that Jesus is the Messiah. *Acts 5: 17 - 42*

Philip and the Ethiopian
Now an angel of the Lord said to Philip, "Go south to the road - the desert road - that goes down from Jerusalem to Gaza." So he started out, and on his way he met an Ethiopian eunuch, an important official in charge of all the treasury of the Kandake (which means "queen of the Ethiopians").

This man had gone to Jerusalem to worship, and on his way home was sitting in his chariot reading the Book of Isaiah the prophet. The Spirit told Philip, "Go to that chariot and stay near it."

Then Philip ran up to the chariot and heard the man reading Isaiah the prophet. "Do you understand what you are reading?" Philip asked.

"How can I," he said, "unless someone explains it to me?" So he invited Philip to come up and sit with him. This is the passage of Scripture the eunuch was reading:

"He was led like a sheep to the slaughter, and as a lamb before its shearer is silent, so he did not open his mouth. In his humiliation he was deprived of justice. Who can speak of his descendants? For his life was taken from the earth."

The eunuch asked Philip, "Tell me, please, who is the prophet talking about, himself or someone else?" Then Philip began with that very passage of Scripture and told him the good news about Jesus.

As they travelled along the road, they came to some water and the eunuch said, "Look, here is water. What can stand in the way of my being baptized?" And he gave orders to stop the chariot. Then both Philip and the eunuch went down into the water and Philip baptized him.

When they came up out of the water, the Spirit of the Lord suddenly took Philip away, and the eunuch did not see him again, but went on his way rejoicing. Philip, however, appeared at Azotus and travelled about, preaching the gospel in all the towns until he reached Caesarea - *Acts 8: 26 – 40*

Cornelius Calls for Peter

In the tenth chapter of the book of the Acts of the Apostles, the following was recorded. At Caesarea there was a man named Cornelius, a centurion in what was known as the Italian Regiment. He and all his family were devout and God-fearing; he gave generously to those in need and prayed to God regularly.

One day at about three in the afternoon he had a vision. He distinctly saw an angel of God, who came to him and said, "Cornelius!"

Cornelius stared at him in fear. "What is it, Lord?" he asked. The angel answered, "Your prayers and gifts to the poor have come up as a memorial offering before God. Now send men to Joppa to bring back a man named Simon who is called Peter. He is staying with Simon the tanner, whose house is by the sea."

When the angel who spoke to him had gone, Cornelius called two of his servants and a devout soldier who was one of his attendants. [8] He told them everything that had happened and sent them to Joppa.

Peter's Vision

About noon the following day as they were on their journey and approaching the city, Peter went up on the roof to pray. He became hungry and wanted something to eat, and while the meal was being prepared, he fell into a trance.

He saw heaven opened and something like a large sheet being let down to earth by its four corners. It contained all kinds of four-footed animals, as well as reptiles and birds. Then a voice told him, "Get up, Peter. Kill and eat."

"Surely not, Lord!" Peter replied. "I have never eaten anything impure or unclean." The voice spoke to him a second time, "Do not call anything impure that God has made clean."

This happened three times, and immediately the sheet was taken back to heaven. While Peter was wondering about the meaning of the vision, the men sent by Cornelius found out where Simon's house was and stopped at the gate.

They called out, asking if Simon who was known as Peter was staying there.

While Peter was still thinking about the vision, the Spirit said to him, "Simon, three[a] men are looking for you. So get up and go downstairs. Do not hesitate to go with them, for I have sent them."

Peter went down and said to the men, "I'm the one you're looking for. Why have you come?" The men replied, "We have come from Cornelius the centurion. He is a righteous and God-fearing man, who is respected by all the Jewish people. A holy angel told him to ask you to come to his house so that he could hear what you have to say." Then Peter invited the men into the house to be his guests.

Peter at Cornelius's House

The next day Peter started out with them, and some of the believers from Joppa went along. The following day he arrived in Caesarea. Cornelius was expecting them and had called together his relatives and close friends. As Peter entered the house, Cornelius met him and fell at his feet in reverence. But Peter made him get up. "Stand up," he said, "I am only a man myself."

While talking with him, Peter went inside and found a large gathering of people. He said to them: "You are well aware that it is against our law for a Jew to associate with or visit a Gentile. But God has shown me that I should not call anyone impure or unclean. So when I was sent for, I came without raising any objection. May I ask why you sent for me?"

Cornelius answered: "Three days ago I was in my house praying at this hour, at three in the afternoon. Suddenly a man in shining clothes stood before me and said, 'Cornelius, God has heard your prayer and remembered your gifts to the poor. Send to Joppa for Simon who is called Peter. He is a guest in the home of Simon the tanner, who lives by the sea.' So I sent for you immediately, and it was good of you to come. Now we are all here in the presence of God to listen to everything the Lord has commanded you to tell us."

Then Peter began to speak: "I now realize how true it is that God does not show favouritism but accepts from every nation the one who fears him and does what is right. You know the message God sent to the people of Israel, announcing the good news of peace through Jesus Christ, who is Lord of all.

You know what has happened throughout the province of Judea, beginning in Galilee after the baptism that John preached - how God anointed Jesus of Nazareth with the Holy Spirit and power, and how he went around doing good and healing all who were under the power of the devil, because God was with him.

"We are witnesses of everything he did in the country of the Jews and in Jerusalem. They killed him by hanging him on a cross, but God raised him from the dead on the third day and caused him to be seen. He was not seen by all the people, but by witnesses whom God had already chosen— by us who ate and drank with him after he rose from the dead.

He commanded us to preach to the people and to testify that he is the one whom God appointed as judge of the living and the dead. All the prophets testify about him that everyone who believes in him receives forgiveness of sins through his name."

While Peter was still speaking these words, the Holy Spirit came on all who heard the message. The circumcised believers who had come with Peter were astonished that the gift of the Holy Spirit had been poured out even on

Gentiles. For they heard them speaking in tongues and praising God.

Then Peter said, "Surely no one can stand in the way of their being baptized with water. They have received the Holy Spirit just as we have." So he ordered that they be baptized in the name of Jesus Christ. Then they asked Peter to stay with them for a few days.

An Angel appeared to Paul during the Storm
After they had gone a long time without food, Paul stood up before them and said: "Men, you should have taken my advice not to sail from Crete; then you would have spared yourselves this damage and loss. But now I urge you to keep up your courage, because not one of you will be lost; only the ship will be destroyed.

Last night an angel of the God to whom I belong and whom I serve stood beside me and said, 'Do not be afraid, Paul. You must stand trial before Caesar; and God has graciously given you the lives of all who sail with you.' So keep up your courage, men, for I have faith in God that it will happen just as he told me. Nevertheless, we must run aground on some island."
Acts 27: 21 – 26

Angel appeared to Zechariah
It was "in the days of King Herod of Judea," says the Gospel of Luke, that the angel Gabriel appeared to an elderly man named Zechariah, a member of the "priestly order of Abijah" who served God in the Temple (Luke 1:5). ... Your wife Elizabeth will bear you a son, and you will name him John" (Luke 1:13)

Angel appears to John

I, John, am the one who heard and saw these things. And when I had heard and seen them, I fell down to worship at the feet of the angel who had been showing them to me. *Revelation 22:8*

Daniel in the lion's den

In the days of his royal Darius the Mede, Daniel was raised to high office because the attempt on his life failed. Daniel's rivalries tricked Darius into making a declaration that for thirty days no prayers should be addressed to any other entity but Darius himself.

It was decreed that anyone who violates the rule will be thrown into the lion's den. Daniel continues to offer supplication unto the God and the king, reluctantly condemn Daniel to death, for the edicts of the Medes and Persians cannot be altered. Hoping for Daniel's deliverance, he has him cast into the den. Early the next morning the king rushed to the place to find out if God had saved his trusted comrade.

Daniel replies that his God had sent an Angel to close the jaws of the lions, "because innocence was found blameless before him." The king ordered that those who conspired against Daniel should be thrown into the lion's den in his place with their family members (wives and children), and that the whole world should worship the God of Daniel.

Shadrach, Meshach, and Abednego

These three men were heroic figures from the third chapter of the Book of Daniel. The three Hebrew men were thrown into a fiery furnace by the Babylonian King Nebuchadnezzar, for failure to bow down to the king's own image.

The three are preserved from harm and the king saw a fourth person walking in the flames with them. According to the King, "the fourth looked like a son of God" – that is an Angel of God.

The first six chapters of the book of Daniel are stories dating from the late Persian/early Hellenistic period. This story has a striking resemblance with the story of Daniel in lion's den. Both stories tend to make the point that the God of the Jews will deliver those who are faithful in worshiping Him.

What is the role of angels when people die?

The Rich Man and Lazarus
The Angels have to navigate the souls of the departed to their correct destination. The scriptures recorded that; "There was a rich man who was dressed in purple and fine linen and lived in luxury every day. At his gate was laid a beggar named Lazarus, covered with sores and longing to eat what fell from the rich man's table. Even the dogs came and licked his sores.

"The time came when the beggar died and the angels carried him to Abraham's side. The rich man also died and was buried. In Hades, where he was in torment, he looked up and saw Abraham far away, with Lazarus by his side. So he called to him, 'Father Abraham, have pity on me and send Lazarus to dip the tip of his finger in water and cool my tongue, because I am in agony in this fire.'

"But Abraham replied, 'Son, remember that in your lifetime you received your good things, while Lazarus received bad things, but now he is comforted here and you are in agony. And besides all this, between us and you a great chasm has been set in place, so that those who want to go from here to you cannot, nor can anyone cross over from there to us.'

The Angel carried the righteous to Abraham's bosom, Paradise side of Hades - *Luke 16:19-23*

What will be the role of angels at the judgment?
God is just: He will pay back trouble to those who trouble you and give relief to you who are troubled, and to us as well. This will happen when the Lord Jesus is revealed from heaven in blazing fire with his powerful angels - *2 Thess. 1:7*

The Son of Man will send out his angels, and they will weed out of his kingdom everything that causes sin and all who do evil. They will throw them into the blazing furnace, where there will be weeping and gnashing of teeth.

Then the righteous will shine like the sun in the kingdom of their Father. Whoever has ears, let them hear. This is how it will be at the end of the age. The angels will come and separate the wicked from the righteous. The angels will gather out of the kingdom all things that offend - *Matthew 13:41- 43, 49*

For it is time for judgment to begin with God's household; and if it begins with us, what will the outcome be for those who do not obey the gospel of God? And, "If it is hard for the righteous to be saved, what will become of the ungodly and the sinner? 1 Peter 4:17

Angels can influence human lives through dreams.

Angels took care of Jacob in all his troubles."Then *the Angel of God spoke to me* in a dream, saying, 'Jacob.' And I said, 'Here I am.' - *Genesis 31:11*

But *God had come to Laban* the Syrian in a dream by night, and said to him, "Be careful that you speak to Jacob neither good nor bad." - *Genesis 31:24*

And Laban said to Jacob "It is in my power to do you harm, but *the God of your father spoke to me last night,* saying, 'Be careful that you speak to Jacob neither good nor bad.' - *Genesis 31:29*

"Unless the God of my father, the God of Abraham and the Fear of Isaac, had not been with me, surely now you would have sent me away empty-handed. God has seen my affliction and the labor of my hands, and rebuked you last night." - *Genesis 31:42*

5 KNOWING THE ANGELS

- *Get to know the four, seven and the twelve Archangels*

According to the first verse of the seventh chapter of Revelation, the Scriptures recorded thatas follows: "After this I saw Four Angels standing at the Four Corners of the Earth, holding back the Four Winds". Here is the Judeo/Christian Interpretation of this Revelation.

'Four Angels' = Raphael, Gabriel, Uriel, Michael
'Four Elements' = Air, Water, Earth, Fire
'Four Corners' = East, West, North, South
'Four Winds' = East Wind of the Morning, West Wind of the Evening, North Wind of Midnight, South Wind of Noon

According to the second verse of the eighth chapter of Revelation "And I saw the seven angels who stand before God, and seven trumpets were given to them". Here are the seven Archangels and their days of jurisdiction.

Michael (Sunday), Gabriel (Monday), Raphael (Tuesday), Uriel (Wednesday), Selaphiel (Thursday), Raquel (Friday), and Barachiel (Saturday).

The most notable reference to a group of seven Archangels appears to have been borrowed from the Jewish **Pseudepigrapha**, namely the 2 BC Book of the Watchers, which at some point was merged with some other books in what is known today as *1 Enoch* (the Book of Enoch), and was made part of the Ethiopian Christian movement scriptural cannon.

At the time it was rejected by Christian leaders from all other denominations as canonical scripture, and despite having been prevalent in Jewish and early Christian Apostolic traditions (as well as the early **Christian leaders** writings) the book just fell from academic and religious status in regards to the rest of the canonical scripture, resulting in the text not being found in most parts of the World, as it was forbidden, from 7th Century AD onwards.

The list of Angels survived only as part of oral traditions that differed to one another depending on the geographical area that they were present, and thus many different lists of angels (termed **"Archangels"**) exist, but to different levels of acceptance.

Here are the twelve Archangels:

Angels are with us all the time. Even when we think we are alone. They hear and see everything we do and think. It's essential for their work. They patiently wait for us to develop. Remember that our guardian angels are here to assist us only, whereas the archangels are here to attend to humanity.

They have special skills related to specific field of undertaking and anyone can call upon them for help in that particular field. We can ask for help from our guardian angels or archangels by communicating with themas detailed in chapter six.

Michael — *"Who is like unto God?"* Daniel.10:13; 12:1; Jude v. 9; Revelation. 12:7-8.

Gabriel — *"The Powerful or Strong Man of God," "The Power or Strength of God"* Daniel.8:16;9:21; Luke1:19-26.
Also called Djibril or Jibril.

Raphael — *"The Healing of God"* Tobit3:17;12:15. Also called Israfel.

Uriel — *"The Light or Fire of God"* A.V. II Esdras 4:1.
Also called Sariel, Suriel, or Muriel.

Selaphiel— *"The Command, Communicant or Prayer of God"*, since command and prayer represent the two forms, or types, of communication: the first one being descendant and the second ascendant.
Also called Salathiel, Selathiel, Seraphiel, Sarakiel, Saraqael, Zarachiel, Zerachiel, or Zachariel.

Raguel — *"The Friend of God."*
Also called Raziel, which means "The Secrets of God."
Not to be confused with Raphael.

Barachiel — *"The Benediction or Blessings of God."*
Also called Varachiel.

Jedudiel — *"The Glory, Laudation or Praise of God."*
Also called Jegudiel or Gudiel.

Jeremiel — *"The Compassion, Exaltation or Mercy of God"* R.V. II Esdras4:36.
Also called Jeramiel, Jerahmiel, Jerehmiel, Ramiel, or Remiel.

Anael — *"The Grace or Joy of God."*
Also called Aniel, Hanael, or Haniel.

Jophiel — *"The Beauty of God."*
Also called Orifiel, Jouphiel, Zouphiel, Zophiel, Zophkiel, Zaphiel, Zaphkiel, Kaphziel, Cassiel, or Kepharel.

Zadkiel — *"The Justice, Righteousness or Uprightness of God."*
Also called Sachiel, Tzadkiel, Zadakiel, Zedekiel, or Zedekul.

6 COMMUNICATING WITH ANGELS

How do I connect with my guardian Angel?
The thing about Angels is that they will find you, more easily than you can find them. They will manifest around you when the time is right, when they are needed, and when you are receptive to their guidance.

That said, prayers and holding an inner focus will help you to open the doors to communications with your Angels. Here is a very effective prayer and visualization exercise to help you:

Take a few big deep breaths, clear your mind and focus on the Creator of all things, then see yourself walking around the heavenly, a lovely breeze rippling through the environment, sun dappling the path in front of you. A perfect day. Ahead you hear a waterfall and just then your path opens up to show you a lovely pool with a waterfall splashing down over the rocks.

There is a large rock on the side of the pool, inviting you to step over and leave your clothes there… and so you do, and you jump into the water, warm and soothing… you swim around for a few minutes and then move over to stand under the falls so you can let the water splash over your body… as it does, you feel yourself releasing all of your cares, you are feeling lighter and lighter, brighter and brighter, more wholly yourself.

After a few minutes you jump back into the pool and swim over to the rock. You notice someone standing by the rock, beckoning you, holding a warm towel for you. You reach for the towel and wrap yourself in it as you both settle on the rock together.

Take a moment to sit together peacefully, to feel the anointing that is moving between you. This is your guardian Angel, ask if this Angel has a name you can use, and listen for a moment, trust whatever comes… and if nothing comes, trust that a name may not be needed, but notice all that happens around you and between you.

Ask your Angel what message they have for you in that moment and again, look around you, listen carefully notice every detail, everything that appears in such an encounter has meaning, symbolism.

Trust that your imagination knows what it's doing in this moment, relax and absorb it. Ask the Angel if they will take a walk with you, and then follow along, see where you go…

Take as much time as you need, ask whatever questions come to mind, and then give the Angel time to respond. When you are finished, walk back to the rock with your Angel(s), thank them for coming to you and invite them to come again, to walk along with you in life.

Then thank God for the experience, take a few deep breaths and come back to yourself. It can be useful at this point to write down what you saw and felt, a way of helping you to assimilate the experience. Pay attention over the next few days, you will probably notice something of an internal shift, new opening and opportunities may present themselves to you after such an encounter.

How can I work and get directions from my guardian Angels?
Once you make that first connection with your Angels, you will want to create other opportunities to connect, but these connections need to have a purpose. It is important to understand that Angels are guardians, not bosses, not even leaders, but guides. Their purpose is to shed light on your path, to give you insights and information that will help you make good decisions.

Most of all their primary function is to help us heal, to help us to look within so we can see what we are doing, thinking or feeling that is hindering us. If an Angel tells you what you should do, you are probably not working with a real Angel.

Remember we have good Angels, bad Angels and the ugly Angels. Good Angels – that is the holy one of God - have no ego, they do not judge us – which also means that they don't give us a lot of confusing or egoistic directives - so if you have an Angel who keeps boosting your ego, you probably don't have a good one.

Angels will always be loving and encouraging, but they will also encourage you to be real, and grounded. They show us where change is desirable, and even how we can make the changes, and they will often help us to attract whatever resources we need to accomplish our goals. But if they insist that you follow their direction, you definitely do not have a good Angel.

One of the first messages that my guardian Angels gave me as we opened the direct communications was that I needed to learn as much as possible about reading the universal signs and symbols.

Angels speak with us in many ways – you are searching for a book, and one just falls off the shelf on your toe- that's probably the book you are looking for and your Angel in action.

Getting answers and insights from your guides is really just a matter of learning to ask the questions and then to notice their communications. The answers may come in a dream, through a song, a movie or a book that falls on your toe, or through a friend you encounter, or a stranger you run into at the bank… Ask a question, ask for help, and then watch, listen, and trust that the answers will come when you need them.

- *Signs, Coincidences and Synchronicity*

When you invite the angels into your life, the world around you changes, it becomes anointed. You enter into a flow of life where coincidences and synchronicities become your clues, leading you to the answer to your prayers. The angels know exactly how to get your attention. So, get ready for some fun! The angels love to playand they want you to know beyond any doubt that they are here to guide you and assist in any and every way they can.

Angels' Nudges

Have you been asking the angels to help you? If so, it's time to start learning how they might be trying to get your attention so they can guide you to the answers you are seeking. The angels are always working behind the scenes in your favour. Sometimes it's through gentle nudges. For example, you're stuck, and you need a sitter for the kids.

You pray to the angels for help and minutes later your friend calls and offers to take your kids. Think about it: Maybe the angels planted your name in her thoughts so she would call you.

Other times the nudge might bonk you over the head. For example, you know the next step in your career is to get certified in a certain specialty and you ask your angels for help because you need the finances to pay for the course. Within the next week, you receive an unexpected check in the mail that covers the expense of the entire course.

The angels love to help and they are always working behind the scenes in your favour. Sometimes it's in small ways and other times it seems like a miracle. Be open to all their loving nudges and get ready to experience the magic of heaven on earth unfolding before your very eyes.

What Is Synchronicity?

Synchronicity is a coincidental occurrence of two or more events that have no relevance to one another, yet when it takes place it has great meaning to the person who is witnessing or experiencing it. The person who experiences a synchronistic event has previously said a prayer or they had a thought or a dream that later comes to fruition.

They witness something that confirms what once was only an image or thought in their psyche. When this happens to you, you need to pay attention. This may be a form of divine communication where the angels are trying to give you a message or they want your attention.

When you walk the spiritual path and you become more conscious, you realize everything happens for a reason. So, a synchronicity is no accident.

The angels use synchronicity to awaken you to their presence and guidance.

Carl Jung coined the term synchronicity and defined it as a meaningful coincidence. The Angels use synchronicity to awaken you to their presence and guidance.

7 FALLEN ANGELS

Lucifer went to the Garden of Eden; deceived Adam and Eve to disobey God and eat the forbidden fruit. This has brought pain and death to the earth inhabitants – Genesis 3

At the onset of the universe, God created the Angels, Archangels, Principalities, Powers, Virtues, Dominions, Thrones, Cherubim and Seraphim. The renowned angels

Gabriel and Michael were among these magnificent beings. But there was yet another entity who stood-out due to his beauty and splendor. He was the most important creature God had ever created and his name is Lucifer.

Lucifer was a magnificent being, a brilliant personality with lots of outstanding qualities and as such pride crept in. Pride is a vice that leads to arrogance, vanity and endless conceit. Remember thatpride was one of the seven deadly sins, so the now proud Lucifer considered himself to be so perfect that he decided to create his own throne placed even above God since he wished to be like God.

To fulfill his heart's desire, Lucifer deceived some angels around him making him the father of mendacity and deception. His deceived about a third of the angels to join his rebellion against God.

And so battle ensued in heaven between the forces of light and the forces of darkness; between the Angels of God and the servants of Lucifer – demons.

How you have fallen from heaven,
morning star, son of the dawn!
You have been cast down to the earth,
you who once laid low the nations!
You said in your heart,
*"**I will** ascend to the heavens;*
***I will** raise my throne*
above the stars of God;
***I will** sit enthroned on the mount of assembly,*
on the utmost heights of the North.
***I will** ascend above the tops of the clouds;*
***I will** make myself like the Most High." (Isaiah 14:12-14)*

Lucifer encountered stupendous antagonist in Archangel Michael who commanded the heavenly militia of God. In the face of this fierce opposition, Lucifer turned himself into a mighty dragon and dueled against Michael who wielded a flaming sword.

Lucifer, like Adam, had a choice. He could accept that God was God or he could choose to decide that he would be god unto himself. His repeated "I wills"? show that he chose to defy God and declared himself to be 'Most High'. A passage in Ezekiel gives a parallel account of the fall of Lucifer:

You were in Eden, the garden of God.
… I ordained and anointed you
as the mighty angelic guardian.
You had access to the holy mountain of God
and walked among the stones of fire.
"You were blameless in all you did
from the day you were created
until the day evil was found in you.
… and you sinned.
So I banished you in disgrace
from the mountain of God.
I expelled you, O mighty guardian,
from your place among the stones of fire.
Your heart was filled with pride
because of all your beauty.
Your wisdom was corrupted
by your love of splendour.
So I threw you to the ground. (Ezekiel 28:13-17)

Notwithstanding all his strength the dragon was defeated by Michael – because God is on his side. Lucifer and his evil angels (hereinafter will be referred to as demons) were banished from Heaven. These demons fell on the earth and have been ensnared in the peripheries of the universe.

Because of pride the once most beautiful angel was transformed into the heinous Satan - Lucifer.
Determined to avenge himself against his creator, Lucifer decided to attack the greatest creation of God - humanity

itself which had been created in the image and likeness of God.

Transforming himself in the likeness of a serpent, Lucifer entered the Garden of Eden and convinced the innocent Eve to taste the forbidden fruit and using his deceitful tongue Lucifer concatenated the original sin which caused Adam and Eve to be driven out of paradise.

 Since then till now, Satan has devoted all his efforts to alienate men from God, turning them into sinners so that they failed to reach paradise. Lucifer the fallen angel rejected God's grace and therefore will spend eternity in a place of isolation.

Why did Lucifer revolt against God?

But why would Lucifer want to confront and commandeer the leadership from the One Omniscient, Omnipotent and Omnipresent Creator? I think Lucifer has failed to do his mathematics right, to work out the potential strength of the opponent before commencing the battle. Common sense dictates that his limited creature-power would have been insufficient for a successful revolt against his Creator.

I wonder why Satan risked all and go into a battle he could not win? I would think that an intelligent Angel would recognize his limitations to challenge his Creator – Omniscience, Omnipotence and Omnipresence – the triune God. Can the move to revolt against God be justified in any way, form or shape?

 This question is puzzling and mind blowing for many. I am still searching to find a more intelligible explanation and the search leads me to the question

"why did God create Satan"?

Well God created Satan as Lucifer, the highest ranking angel of all. Lucifer, however, wasn't content to worship and serve his Creator. Full of pride, he rebelled, leading a third of the angels away from God. Unable to match the Almighty God, Lucifer was cast to the earth where he has operated as the devil ever since.

God did not create Lucifer as evil but allowed the potential for sin. While God cannot commit sin, He doesn't take it away from those who do. When Lucifer chose to rebel, he instantly became the author of sin. Evil is the result of a free-will choice by Lucifer.

After being baptized by John the Baptist, Jesus was tempted by the devil for 40 days and

nights in the Judaean Desert. During this time, Satan came to Jesus and tried to tempt him – Matthew 4: 1 - 11

ABOUT THE AUTHOR

I am a father of two boys and two girls, and have been happily married for over three decades. I am a senior Anglican Clergyman and part time Hospital Chaplain.

This book is the result of my years of experience as a servant in the Lord's vineyard. I enjoy teaching and transferring the knowledge that I have acquired over the years to people to lighten their spirit and help them to accomplish more in life.

I pass on the knowledge in this book in the hope that it finds a receptive reader in you, and acts as a catalyst, even if just in some small way, to help you along on your journey of exploration.